SPIRIT UNDER CONSTRUCTION

JERRY HARP

D1601049

NeoPoiesisPress.com

NeoPoiesis Press, LLC

2775 Harbor Ave SW, Suite D, Seattle, WA
Info@NeoPoiesisPress.com
NeoPoiesisPress.com

Copyright © 2017 by Jerry Harp

All rights reserved. No part of this book may be used or reproduced in any manner whatsoever without express written permission from the publisher except in the case of brief quotations embodied in critical articles and reviews.

Jerry Harp – Spirit Under Construction
ISBN 978-0-9975021-7-6 (paperback: alk. paper)

1. Poetry. I. Harp, Jerry. II. Spirit Under Construction.

Library of Congress Control Number: 2017955327

Design, art direction & typography: Milo Duffin and Stephen Roxborough
Cover photograph by Stephen Roxborough

Printed in the United States of America

*This book is dedicated with love
to Mary Szybist.*

contents

section III

section IV

"Here is
the moment
when translation
begins"

Houses

They've been around in dreams a long time now,
those houses where nobody lives, hidden
along long stretches of field, accessible
if you run alone down dirt and gravel roads

late in the afternoon when shadows start
to sift like sand. I think you'll know the place
better than I. Maybe you'll finish this poem.
Here's my attempt to hand it over to you.

The time. The place. The sound. They fade from me
as my pen scratches across the ragged page
and the cat lounges, observing every move.
By the time I climb the stairs to sit before

my glowing screen, how many days and years
will have gone by? But only you will know.
Someone is sitting by an upstairs window,
head bent beside a desk lamp, writing. You knock.

No other houses show. There is no answer.
You cross the dusty living room. A grove
of alder trees, entwined with vines, appears
out back—on the mantle, a clock without a face.

The crickets scrape their stridulation from
the shade. The nighthawk with its plaintive cry
and rush of wings appears at the right time.
Nothing stirs upstairs. You look in every room.

The moonlight shines through a far window. Now
the poem begins. The anticipated turn.
The much awaited answer from the trees.
Here is the moment when translation begins.

GOING ALONG

I'm thinking about the old farm again,
the humid summer rows like fields of hell
where I planted a weed hook in my shin.
It wasn't like I lived there,

but I escaped anyway, went every direction
the compass could conceive. Dusty and tired
along the road, I met a woman once or twice
but hardly need to say how that turned out.

I think, therefore I'm thinking more,
and every time I'm starting out, there's something
brings me back—a little rain, the flapping geese,
the neighbor's Newfie like a leashed bear cub.

All this rain then hail and snow becomes
a vision of hereafter with leaves and cars
and darting wings. I almost didn't come back,
but then I came back.

The doctor recommends some tranquil recollection.
Searching and searching, I've tried to stop,
but it's a real no-go on stopping.
The neighbors' dogs give meaningful looks.

Meanwhile, my paperwork is in.
The only thing's to go back where I came.
Trouble is, that's an expanding blank
with an even blanker blank inside.

That must be where I'm from.
Fill in the blank, and I'm no longer home.
So let this going along get going along.
I could tell you stories, like the time

I slept... but there I go again,
like a bawdy economy coming unregulated.
Let's put this intimate future on reverb.
The dog across the street turned around twice

then sniffed my way and lay in the shade.
I barely know how to be in touch again.
I'll go on. This is to no one in particular.
I'll wait while everything dies.

MY MOTHer'S BeDTIme STOrY

The emperor turned to tyranny.
Even so, he couldn't get his way.
Giant annelids entered the realm.

The size of human arms, of legs,
they burrowed deep in the mud
and broke through the marble

of the palace and grand plaza.
The royal lions pursued them
but could never subdue them.

The gardener found two lions
lounging underwater
beside an annelid at rest,

guarding it like a companion.
How they learned to breathe down there
no one ever discovered,

nor did the subjects of the realm
bend to the emperor's demands,
but rather waded into the water

and breathed a new language erasing
the emperor's decrees, erasing
the palace, the plaza, and the realm.

THE GOSPEL ACCORDING TO BATMAN

In the Batcave I was born again
over and over twice a week—

the colored lights and constant hum,
the music of cold, dark stone,

it was a catacomb of fighting all the wrong.

With a bath towel safety-pinned around my neck,
I ran into the world that was the world
I could become in all those dreams,

>   the activation that the stone
>   revealed, the BIFF! the ZAM! the POW!

At night I looked up, learning the stars.
Bruce Wayne knew their many names.

>   Blessed are those deadpan lines....

>   "Of what use is a dream if not a blueprint
>   for courageous action."

>   "Some days you just can't get rid of a bomb."

Don't hide your lights, the hum.

They were an OOF-KAPOWIE pair
running deep in that device
that was the world clutching the roots that clenched.

ocean

It was an all-day query. I rafted
the shoreline discoveringly. A ship
traced the horizon like déjà vu

the first time ever. I was ten.
The waves kept asking the same question.
Tan children screamed answers.

A snorkel rose from the shallows, the mask
behind it a creature from a foreign realm.
I stayed to myself, drifting in solitudes

I shared with the gulls and one pelican
riding the nearby swells. What kind of creature
was I? I didn't yet know to ask.

Brother to the shells along the shore—ridged,
sand-crusted, silent—I took my meaning
into a flattened present where no history

worried its frayed edges. Inhuman,
anonymous, I waited for nothing.
Nor did my ridges speak lesser tales.

My parents turned on a late movie,
but even Bogart in his darkest scenes
had nothing on a night edged in sand.

I cashed in my sunsets for a torrid zone
without a past. What scents and et ceteras
could this world yet provide?

WORKING FOR MY UNCLE

That's the boss man.
He's a big bang-bang man
with languid eyes and a smooth stride,
his cock-of-the-walk-
hey-look-at-me walk.
He says, Pick up the pace. Says,
Let your legs swing free
when you carry that board.
Andy's my partner in deliveries.
We made our way east,
took a hard right, went down to the river,
and there was Boss Man
with his brand new boat
and his belly shining white in the sun.
He offered us a ride
all the way to Kentucky.
How could we decline?
It was our job to please the boss.
He took us to a sand bar
and left us for the night.
Next morning we showed up late.
The boss delivered an oration—
caustic, crude, and orotund—
saved up for the occasion.
We smelled like river mud.
That was the day that Andy,
a fair-haired boy destined for more
than the boss could offer,
quit. It was an infernal time that day
delivering couches alone,
but the boss said it could be done.
I hear he sits in his house alone
where boxes, dust, and dirty dishes pile up.
His store is long ago gone.

American CHILDHOOD

The only madeleine I ever found
was the drainage ditch behind our house,
sewage and leaves drifting into the woods
where mayflies hovered in the heat
and cicadas tuned themselves all afternoon,
so when I pass that corner where the yards
hold standing water, I'm off in woods again,
grabbing a grape vine, swinging above
a creek so placid that it stands in mud.

Kids from the neighborhood ran down the block
where blackberry vines clung to the trees along
an empty lot where we filled our Mason jars.
When poison oak erupted up my arms,
the couch became my refuge for a week.
Dad took me for my first library card.
I spent the next week studying fingerprints
and tracking diagrams in the detective handbook
I carried with me night and day.
We walked down to the river and threw
rocks in the water and collected shells
before he stopped at the Legion for a beer,
while at my table I drank an orange crush.
At night I washed the shells and lined
them up along my windowsill.

My father faked repairing factory machines
until he trained apprentices in his trade.
I knew I'd come of age when he showed
me how to cut the grass. The summer passed
like shadows lengthening across the lawn.
But then those other kids kept coming by,
who didn't dress or smell like us.

We chased them off our streets, or tried.
They rode their rusted bikes to where we didn't know.
My father might have said, except
he died like a winter night.
My uncle said there's always something fathers
and sons can talk about, but Dad,
propped in his hospital bed, said
that there was nothing he could say.

Evenings, I jog along the woods and search
the creeks for clues to how I might have answered.
The nighthawks, diving, cry,
and in the ditches frogs play their metallic music
like a lawnmower sputtering grass, rust, and smoke.

More about working for my uncle

Cross-hatched, repurposed, I rave.
The reports are in: I'm erratic.
The managers gather in their enclave.

At least I'm something—angry and demotic.
As Marx said, "Why fuck around with second-rate talent?"
I used to be exotic,

but refinement throws me off balance.
Right now? The second hand ticks and tocks.
More Goofus than Gallant,

I pratfall for blocks.
How much do the managers get for rent,
and what for local artifacts?

Whatever it is, I'm against it. Dependent
on official translations, blue fires
sucking like mouths pursue every descendent,

burning toward apocalypse. I'll hire
a new lawyer once I learn to haunt
more bitter memories and ires.

Their language nauseates my weather. Rain taunts
the plaza's tesserae
while jokes accompany devotional chants.

I'm holding out for a better cliché.
This is no life for a conscious man.
It gets late earlier every day.

Remembrance

Wanting to know what I crawled—moss,
streambed, gravel. Crossed? Cursed.
What fungi could cover me?
I have some words for them, if there

are any words left. My hand hurts.
My head is going numb.
Just another day on the terrace.
From here the outbuilding shows, the roof

just beyond those trees, where they wouldn't
let me out for weeks.
Some Mother-Father type, they
drove downtown to drop me off.

Good thing I burrowed back in my closet
beside some shoes and an old dartboard
I whispered to in the dark.
When they finally found me, they burned

with their stares and ironic twists.
It was every ounce of love they had
spilled there on the floor—eyeballs,
smiles, and fingernails congealing in a world.

River Memory

A teenager sitting by the river,
I was dreaming up this poem.

      I didn't know it yet.

Better to lose myself in that water,
a face dissolving, passing there.

The sunset turned to copper.
That was the poem, after all,
monumental and impoverished.

The moon came out rippling in the tide,
another sleep murmuring there

in someone else's dream telling me
I could write it all down, if I wanted to,

write it all down.

ST Francis OF ASSISI

When I was a frantic teenage fanatic,
walking barefoot in the snow,
going days without food,

and visiting the nursing home,
I thought it was the least I could do.
Francis knew, even if no one else cared.

That year didn't even yield a holy card,
and the birds paid me no mind
no matter how I addressed them.

They were off again even as I stood
like the plastic statue on my bedroom shelf.
When I stretched out on the floor at night,

my dog (faithful as the Wolf of Gubbio)
stared longingly at the bed,
but sighed and settled at my side.

Francis took the wolf by the paw
and struck a deal—he had a way
with bad boys, having been one himself.

But he had to get going, there being
a church to reform, beggars to feed,
and lepers to bathe, not to mention

his new digs in a cave outside town.
I had to get going too, off to college
for a year too obsessed with sin

to sit for long and read.
I lay on the floor at night.
What was I looking for?

The weather had other plans for me.

ELSEWHERE

You, always there before thought,
other myself and to, and there,
if I stopped believing, would the moon
shine more brightly? Would you reach me?

The river curves its question, running
beside the traffic, headlights coming on.
I find myself elsewhere, always
before attention begins, then elsewhere again

beyond the elsewheres I've named.
Now that I'm the age my father was
the year he died, I can stop proving
that I exist. Why do I still ask?

When my father came up the river
as our hometown Santa Claus
in a vehicle that rolled onshore,
I was there beside him, his helper

handing candy canes to children
lining up to tell him their desires.
His death in winter was a thing that happened.
It had nothing to do with me.

FaTHer FaTHer

Striding the college halls, bouncing
on the balls of his feet, his scapular
wilting from his shoulders, he declined

his nouns with conviction,
cited encyclicals from memory,
and kept all his facts straight,

from church history to the poetry he quoted.
He recited Aquinas verbatim.
When he inhaled a cigarette, it stayed inhaled.

"Father, would you mind not smoking in class?"
"This is my class, I'll smoke if I goddamned well please."
Drifting through the room like unfettered ganglia,

he spoke edited prose all week without consulting
a single note, corrected every doctrinal error,
then retired to his office to read Homer in Greek

and annotate the church fathers.
How many of us left his class awed to silence,
or dropped his class, "leaping," he liked to say,

"like rats from a fucking sinking ship,"
the smoke roiling from his mouth to veil his head.
He clipped his consonants and opponents.

Evenings, he whistled out beyond the lake,
filling the woods with his tune.
In one homily he said that if it rained all the time,

eventually we wouldn't notice, and God's grace
is like the rain, and prayer is realizing
you're being rained on. Well.

Brother's Room

Gauze curtains filter sunlight into dust
across the floor and the plastic shards
from a shattered proof-coin case.
The wine-red rug lingers in cigarette smoke.
The record player skips and stutters down.
Goodbye to summer and The Rolling Stones,
goodbye to all those Main Streets and days.
How long could it last anyway?
Welcome the regimes of minor chords,
disjunctive phrases, repeating phrases.
Blood is the red, blood is the go.
Where from here then?
Judges and junkies plot the next chapter.
Is that a hint of ozone in the air?

"I am
the question
I shall not
ask"

THE REPORT

The woman at the window eyed me.
I've come to turn myself in, I said.

She answered, *Your name isn't in the book,*
her voice marble, her blue eyes

as drab as the sky. Touching her shoulder,
I cooled my forehead on her voice.

Consider the accuser, she said.
The clock against the far wall chimed.

She led me to an inner room
where she locked the doors and windows

and took off her clothes. She was hirsute,
fat, and beautiful. She took my hand.

She began reciting this poem.
Clocks all over town were chiming.

Turning

She turned and turned and looked my way,
her eyes shining like glass.
The streetlights buzzed. Smoothing her skirt,
she bared her teeth.
Somewhere inside, a baby cried.
When the streetlight flickered, she sank into a doorway.
Her eyes became a doorway, a shadowed doorway
with peeling paint and wafts of cooking food.
In this doorway a woman stood.
She turned and turned.
A wrapper tumbled across dead grass
as a car with a single headlight passed.
Somewhere inside, a man was calling.
The woman's eyes became a shadowed doorway.
Paper tumbled along the sidewalk
where streetlights buzzed. She bared her teeth.
She turned and turned. Inside, there was a baby's cry,
and in the distance a man was calling.

HIS Mechanical Garden

The machine shines in the grass, the grass
shines in the windows, everything reflects.
The pulleys and cogwheels grind like
there's something more to say. I
have nothing more to say except except.

I greet myself in the shadows as I
limp by, looking all over town for my antithesis,
like a swollen lover about to be found out.

I couldn't take my jerry-built apartment
one more day—is why my things lie
in cold storage and I'm strolling all over again,
like an old man dodging bricks.

                          But I don't worry.
My friend says I can stay as long as
I'm gone by the time she wakes up.
My legs become the fear that nothing will change.

I sneak up on myself over there, under
the chestnut tree, getting sicker
every minute, but I never catch up.

That nixie singing flame means nothing
but the water she draws you to.
I am a horse gliding into the dark.
I am calliope music up and down the river.

FIGure in starLIGHT

From his recliner he stared
at her empty dress. The bell
struck midnight. The windows shook.

When she stepped out of the shower,
a towel wrapped around
her waist, he groaned

and applauded as she paced,
passing the ugly child in
his bed, who observes

this scene in his sleep. Asthmatic, chilled,
he notes the man's stained T-shirt.
I was that man, but now

I am the child tangled in
these gauzy sheets. I mean no harm. I
lie here while everyone breathes.

THE UNNAMED POSSIBLE

Furthermore, any advantage today
goes through the storm drain tonight.
Oh, and a lot more. I'm burning up.
I swerve all over town.

Calls and caws up and down the street
and time. Liberal democracy, goodbye and,
man, traipsing through the streets, I slid,
skidded downhill into traffic. *Humani nihil*

a me... Isn't it better he's not in the world?
the policeman said. Going down,
the sun turned the city hepatitis yellow.
I don't know what to do with vision.

Be the change jangling in your pocket.
It was the father's smoky breath I clung to
that night, dark circles in dark circles.
It was all the brother I had, waking

me up to say the news. I didn't
say anything back. Okay, this
one-way hallway leads I don't know where.
I need a great band and lots of vegetables.

HAYSTACK ROCK,
cannon beach, oregon

It rises to overhang and feather.
It is face and highest form.

What is its name but failed imagination?
One day it will be gone,

but in its own geologic time.
I lean into *wing*, into *fall* and *jut forth*.

Framed by the telescope, a black oyster catcher
sits at the base, its orange beak

pointing into the wind—Chase and Take.
The words sit brooding there.

They ask nothing of us.
Centuries come to them.

Centuries come and go.
Mantras to my run: "edge" and "pointed end."

Along the shore, one monolith
after another stands—dark, brooding, barnacle-
covered.

Stop there long enough,
you'll see a barnacle move in the sun, the slightest
shift,

a foreign realm's illegible communiqué.
The oily, ink-blot waves rush

and rush the shore, as in "shadow."
As in delete, erase, scrape clean.

A BOOK OF Hours

Between two columns without a roof,
I pass my days and nights, clipping

the grass, polishing marble, reading
my books by moonlight.

My sight runs down like a clock.
A gray-eyed Manx comes by at evening.

I feed her from the day's leavings.
She leads me down to the river,

where I scrawl in the sand
and wait for the tide to recede.

I am this Manx's ambivalent other.
I am the time these columns keep.

I wait for something to happen.
I am the question I shall not ask.

Arrival

Driving past walkers, statues, and stores,
past telephone wires and sidewalk inscriptions,

I was looking for you before I knew
the statues and sidewalk inscriptions

and didn't know that I was looking.
I did not stop—the walkers passing by

I did not talk to—driving past stores
and statues, and did not ask directions those years

before I knew the sidewalk inscriptions,
the walkers I was driving by, what

the phone lines there might open to,
driving and looking, the storefronts going by

and walkers passing, stopping to look inside
the windows, catching a glimpse years before

I went out walking and driving,
driving and looking, looking before I knew.

WHere are YOU TakinG me?

There you were saying more,
describing the lore that makes your day run,
roses and myrtle, limelight and hunted shade.

The place, the other place
without language or dreams,
a hunted-for and offered place,
drew your language away from you.

The moon bore down its heavy light,
one revolution and another—
where were you wandering then?
Asleep, why would you care for
the resonant, the grass?

We'll have eternity to brood about it all,
like the lore gone dripping from the skies.
The speaking happens, it comes undone,
and what is coming next, it's what comes next.
Like the grass, don't let the lexicon go.
Don't let it, it echoes.
Don't. It goes.

TWO BOOKS SHE

When she went away and was that distance,
sky and steel,

her absence was the air in every room—
shimmering, shifted—

glitter on the pastry board. She left two books behind.
One was

her handwritten declaration of the body scented
vinegar and clove,

pages under a crescent moon, out walking,
damp shade.

The other was a volume she studied for years
about becoming

someone other. This one she took up when
she returned.

She chanted from it. Her voice came over me,
segmented sleep.

Ambitious Expenditures

Waves crashing against the rocks conjoin
to a coming tide. Together and apart,

we wander the morning, ground coffee
and strolling along. Terns glide between sand

and towering rock, drinking in greens and browns
in solitude formation where cameras take us

and the terns. At night the streets go quiet.
Surveying and othering along, an owl

perches on a neighbor's roof, an open parenthesis
to the creeping mist. The two of us,

the three, look along the sand, outseeing,
the waves emerging to what once was called the soul.

We watch out other theres.

practical theology

Depictions of our arguments come crashing
in the rain. Rats scratch inside the walls.
A branch scraping the house

makes the only sound we sing for days.
It's more than what one does, more yet
than reading the scribbled hand of one

who died in a distant country where
her late, mailed letter lingered somewhere
between the island and landlocked state.

Sometimes, folding the morning paper, you said,
The love of God requires two things:
the preparation and the putting away.

When I try speaking, bird sounds come out,
and the page falls to an alphabet I've not
yet learned to read. Discordant notes.

My answers turn out wrong because
the text is off by one—one sound,
one declension, one breath released.

These missives fall like sand, a sudden
country awakened to in a distant room,
a tarnished ring passed on for centuries.

I don't remember what it means.
There was a letter, but the letter's lost.
The song comes scraping on the stairs.

Bridges & the Impossible Net

It was a rhythm on the cobbled street, a dark
and empty clopping, force and lack shambled
together—old, old, and older—

bridges laced up and together.

This questioning comes up, words and steam,
this questioning, bitter bells turning dust
in all the blue, clopping in daylight,
latticed windows into evening.

The trees were angles that became the trees,
the shapes they occupy, belfries, teenagers
huddled over smartphones and guitars.

"WHATever
IS COMING,
IT'S GOING TO
HAPPEN"

SUNDAY EVENING

Where impromptu tents line the block, shopping carts
and crates, coffee cups, commands,
                    a tarp rustling in the wind,

the post flanking the church door—
            Paz a todos—

"We gather in," she says,

        "the name of…"

We gather in the name, down again and down,
the darkness rising, we're down and down.
We gather in letters saved as in breath,

            in the name of—
coffee and bread, saved and closing down,
we gather in the name of the name.

Next door a band practices. The drums and rain
become the dark, our circle hand to hand, a reading
down books and days, broken and closing down.

By the strip club up the street, what do
those bodies do in tents and drifting in
and out up and down the block?
A policeman checks in, looks over a tarp,
draws some coffee, and goes on.

This morning another shooting.
Yes, we knew him. What news, what darks,
what blues and humming down the down.

It started all over, all over the news,
clearing the sidewalks and streets, the candidates
walking into studios again. The band playing.

Saved as in coming down.
We calm the down. Saved as in walking away.
As in the blue tarp, the blue tent.
Up and down and all along the downs.

credo

I believe in all that. It is a coming to.
It is brass green and becoming,

wooden benches, piled stones.
Already we are reforming.

We bring roses and blue candles, brush remnants
of leaves and red dust into the hall.

We leave off the rituals. The leavings
daisy off the day, the birds and bricks.

Here is a gathering and a going off.
They meet us again. Stern voices in the portico.

Cigarette smoke. Familiar music.
I say, "Easy, pipe, wind."

We weather arrivals past everything.
We shroud the weathered yard,

let it go dry, turn waters elsewhere.
We learn the lines

and make it up as we go,
this dark section of reason and that,

a starry thing rife with eyes,
stumbling into place. Fingers crease,

increase the measure, fretting
the strings. The stringed music plays.

THE DEMONSTRATIONS

By the end of summer, I'd forgotten, almost,
why we were there. More kept coming across the river,
in vans, on foot. On the lawns bodies lounged,

humming hits and old movie tunes, and then it was
the old, familiar chants, and bodies half-naked
and solvent, waving signs—it was all in the wrist,

lovely and ongoing. We were safe-keeping in June.
Jimson weed ran wild behind city hall.
It was sweltering for days, for days and nights

haze hanging over us—pollen, voices, dust.
I remember dark stairways and rooms, meetings,
and never settling on a statement

where a world and a world come on.
We had to yield the place to another sir
who was all about advancing the institution.

How did he wander into us?
It was a coming on and a coming on.
The next generation had not arrived.

The climate could yet recover, but I can't
apply this planet to any other example.
The chants go on. What else is there to do?

It's the gist of what doesn't happen most concerns.
Meet me by the water. Say it. Space is limited.
Let the children decide who dies next.

ELEGY

A chord played over and over. The pain
of just going on, dust and voracious spaces—
that's how it was all day in the streets,

the plaza, angels singing their hymns of liberty
and rice, drugged, Apollonian, appealing
to every artifact and sense they stumbled on.

They breathed their husky mantras in the heat,
multicolored, dragging their feathers along
the stones and trash where one of them asked me

for a handout—but how could I donate
to such a higher creature? All the same,
smelling like cigarettes and beer, its left wing

splendid in the sun, if ragged and worse for wear,
the right one at its feet, what ethereal
confusion shone in its eyes—I've seen that before—

as it shambled past the man playing xylophone
and dogs asleep and all the other
Seraph alleles manifest in blues and greens

morphing into blues; we're animals really—yes?
Vast like an ocean and as salty, the angel
came back to me downcast and other,

saying that death is the only condition.

THE HOUSE

I won't lie, under the trees out that window
they took her decades ago.

We were there all along. We watched it pass.
Years she sat upstairs, head inclined
beside her desk lamp. "Jesus the dear lord vermin,"
she said. Evening or night walking the road,
I saw her up there. Her presence functioned for those
living outside. They waited.
They lined up beside the cemetery.

She came along in blue and incantatory,
a form of boron around here. She gave out
bread and bread and bread. She knew their names.
An old man—I'm sure I knew him once—wandered
room to room looking for that last book he needed
to finish his manuscript; he called her away.
We let him call. They took her
out along the bumptious road—what collars?
What concessions? What drills down?

In the house everything creaks, creaks and sags,
the plumbing backed up and lights failing.
He called her away, and she was away.
It's a bucket of tin soldiers and years in here.
The sensation remains here in my pocket,
the lint I've saved.

Outside is a clarity too clear for stars.
They called her grieving, and she was.

THE RECKONING

It was a loss. And then it was again,
a loss and all over, frequencies

coming in and out, how long can it go on?
Last night they took the body away,

took in linen and away. What connects?
What draws down? What flares?

I doubt that even the cable guy,
bending with his tools and technical acumen,

could detail the day's damages,
the night's fallout. It was a loss,

the mirror's images. It was away.
Sad man, where are you, your little green, your pills?

I re-invoked that other. It is myself I am.
Passing a ball back and forth, we talked

about the body—by then it was away.
We talked in provocation, enjoining

what inceptions the afternoon could muster.
We talked it away. There was a woman wearing

a head scarf, blond in the wind, bending over
the water, in the blond wind bending.

I was looking there, bending. What was bending?
Take the body back, ashen and back. How could I

occupy a space excised on my behalf?
An advantage of the postured mouth.

Leave it to the garbage personnel
to give a summing up, sort through it all.

It was a telling, and it was told.
Dark coverts in a canoe—take the body there.

Is it there, finagled green? Early evenings
remain my only currency, iron darkness

rising and then rising, all that dark.
The postal carrier brought no promise.

The buzz went on through lavender.
Sad man with your little green, where do you linger?

HISTORY & SUN

Splitting sunlight with its angled head,
slowly twisting in the angled light,
a crystal angel sways, suspended by a thread.

The light fades down the walls, an indigo streak
forming a hieroglyph, or something in Greek,

about an underworld where shadows
arrange themselves in shifting formation.

Who could rest easy, being dead?
Like the living, they seek new motivation.

Ten minutes after the hour, the hours chime.
These things are not my obsession,
                        but give them time.

Approaching the age my father died,
I'm learning again to orient the world
as I did when I was a child:
Face the river. West lies to my right.
Fields stretch behind me. Sun rises in the east.

From the shade of cedar trees, my father approaches
with all the petty grandeur of the recently deceased.

Head down, his unzipped jacket flailing in the breeze,
he points to the river, but does not speak.

Leaving

The light, a scar without a backstory,
motivates a traffic in derailments

and calls back windowed rooms with schoolbooks
stained by rain. What guilts are these
that, leaving, grieve? Nothing leads where I'd thought.

Go to the garage. Check the car.
Everything is going to be fine.

Biking to the city, those miles and years—
like if I pedaled long enough, it would become
another where, transport the place,
translucent and aware—I entered these thoughts,
humming in the dark. The story of the going
becomes the going on, the place I go

when I leave the world, all I really know
of this or any world—headlights, departures, doors.

THE EVENT

I'm outside talking to my neighbor
with his dog, Zoe, waiting patiently in the yard
because she knows that soon it's time to eat,
and there's this tremor in the air, strange and gone.

The authorities are in agreement.
It will happen. Every adjunct to every day converges.
There is no turning back.
The doorknobs gleam with its coming.

That day in eighth grade after my father died,
I went out running—I stayed out of school that day—
and ran across some friends walking home for lunch
and wanted to go with them and back to class
and leave the relatives behind, the niceties.

Whatever is coming, it's going to happen.
Breathe. It will be over.
Every doorbell contributes to the tune.
We turn our laptops to the sky.

I ran into an old friend whose aching desire
to do good I find tiresome.
He wouldn't stop talking the weathers.

Today when I walked down the street, a crow
perched on a tall pine and cawed and cawed
like it had something to say.

Heart Prayer

I really over-shared that night,
with tinsel, trinkets, and strings—
it all came out huddled beside
that documentary about a lost boy

proving he was there all over again.
It was a yard with screens, twitches, and blades,
the springs and wheels running down
that ran the mechanism running me,

a broken-livered rhythm coming on
like the fog I breathed when I was six;
I'm losing half an inch a year since then
while others tick and trek along.

The soft-talker I followed all this time
speaks long pauses over rice, and my longing
never ends up belonging, nor does any
other-where ever shine like foil.

Like the old man said: Never stay
where you're welcome. He was right
on cue, his stupefaction coming on
to me, so here I go off script.

I'm my own Linear B, which I can't read.
It was the moon-landing night, the old man
shot cardiac sparks, and sure enough I was next,
out walking fields in mud and rain

somewhere between God and none.
What difference does it make, some tran-
scendental desire suffering the universe
while planets reel in empty space?

Either way, by the time those dots of light
get here, their stars have moved or gone,
and here I drag this thing I am along
with shadows that are me and that are not.

IN TIME

It was a rainy night all the way here.
We walked barefoot through the mud
then left off where the road gave out.
We stood among dripping trees.
If only common sense were less common.

On the porch's tin roof, the rain
took me to the moment among the graves
when we stood around your body,
the fresh dirt and your body,
our voices low among the evergreens.

Can you hear us where you are? Can you
spin the holy hoop? Our circles gave on
to the dirt, the trees, and the games
at the river where three boys drowned
in currents too cold to swim.

Remember them, and us who lack the breath
to recollect ourselves. I've waited by this window
long enough to forget whose house this is,
whose morning paper, coffee, and regrets.
The streets darken in the rain.

TWIN

At night I listen for the whispers of
the one I've always known was there, my dark

companion I would only miss if he
were gone. The doctor said he would remove

the subsumed twin he found, a zodiac
revolving in its own night sky, a tumor

that the specialist, looking at me gravely up
and down, remarked is where the twin resides,

exerting undue pressure on my brain,
but I know I couldn't bear the loneliness.

The voices passing beyond the office door
go into the gray and cannot know the voice

advising every moment, sharp as pins.

VISITING Home after LONG ABSence

I'm a shabby coat sweeping along the street.
I'm slashes in my shoes, and I'm the shoes.
I was a brownstone walkup on a busy street,

but then the tickets came.
I am my own suspension bridge.
There is nowhere I lead, hanging

above a wilderness of highways.
An old tune goes all day. I am
glass hands, root structures in bronze.

The tune burrows in the basement and vibrates
in the walls. It's a robed figure
walking in the fog beside a lake.

A green snake lies coiled on a rock.
Beyond the trees lightning flashes.
I raise my hand to the stone facades, waiting

for words that don't arrive.
I come from a time when gutturals
were the rage, when pelts lined every tongue.

Guitar Lesson

Aquamarine accumulates.
On the horizon is aquamarine.

It spreads to shadow and distance.
St. Bruno leads the way into the woods,

where snow falls for weeks,
driving them all down the mountain.

There they make do and their solitude.
A slow walk. A wall.

A calling. Roots clutch deeper.
In the end is aquamarine.

Tell it again. Start from the beginning,
from before the beginning. Tell it

in aquamarine—the missing minutes,
the archduke on a side street,

footprints on the moon:
it all fades in aquamarine.

Drums pound out the time.
A starling. A crow. A phone ringing

over and over. A dark room. Tell it all.
It is a becoming, a green sound

in a dark, dark night.
A piano piece. A broken string.

Anselm's Others

Syllables drift along, and the air.
Where's all this going?
Oranges, coffee, and late-

night convergences. Believe
and understand the back roads,
the bicycle over gravel.

Let X be...let it,
and not in mind only.
Trawling my vocabulary,

I come up blank every time.
These words are otherwise, left
over from some whereas,

a shelf of entering leaves.
I rode over a wall and let it
be becoming. It was a little

clear-headed, my fall,
a shift of diction, a lalling stage
that never quite came clean.

Whatever is greatest comes after
the greater-than-which, beyond even
selves and selving. Here's the place

where light catches outcroppings,
ice, and monuments too broken
to marry their tonic shadow.

Doctor, what goes across, what shines?

"where
THIS THINKING
GOES IS a SINGED anD
SOLDereD
Guess"

we are seared

together—cauterized, consumed, turned in.
A sullen face glares on the cars up and down

the highways where unshadowed hikers hitch.
We make up stories where they go.

We bring oral formulation into play,
sexual experiment, first impressions, clouds.

You declare, *To the horizon and back.*
Before the first minute, I respond.

We have arrived at this fluorescent place,
a tile floor, one desk, one bed, one chair,

and bells on the quarter hour.
We are a spirit under construction.

What we'll find across the water is yet to be.
The seascape is another memory.

Where this thinking goes is a singed
and soldered guess.

TreLLIs

Stand up, Mary, the world is full of days,
the rain is coming, there are
no flowers for you to hold.

In the margins, sounds of ocean waves
come up, hints of salt on the air,
distant cries and gull cries, a flashing light.

Stand up, Mary, the room's arrangements wait.
This olive branch stands a perfection of waiting
with its slender and oily leaves. The bleached walls

abut long shelves of moldy books, cases
of leather manuscripts beside a leather door.
Stand up, Mary, on the blue porch like a prow

headed to the open sea. The prayer book
falls open to a page I've never seen.
The droning starts up again.

With sidelong looks and slanting mouths,
the babies come for you. They wear
tuxedoes and evening gowns; their rattles shake

the walls. Bullfrogs become the coming rain.
This is your picture, though
no angel sweeps in to point to your desire.

Square and solid, this is your room.
We love you, Mary, we love you.
Stand up and take us in your gaze.

Testament

I give my body to the grass,
the roots, and the weather.

I give my ears to sunlit piercings,
my fingers to the fellowship of clouds.

I toss this dirt across your grave.
To the dirt I give my hands,

to the roses my eyes.
My teeth I give to the wooded path

where I burn myself like incense
and swallow stones instead of bread.

A Letter to God

Other there before and coming as waves
that crash against the shore from the barge
that passed a minute ago riding low on the water,
rocking the rusted dock, the strong brown water
crashing over pebbles and shells, thrashing
the saplings that lean from the shore
down the bluff from the water treatment plant and,
to my left, the shell of the old hominy mill,
the empty bandstand behind me, everything
silent except for the waves and the occasional
car on the street farther up, along
with the constant hum of the world indistinguishable
from the head-hum of the world within.

My pains, penances, and torments—tired.
I'm tired of them all. Let be.

How can I imagine you? Tired
of wanting to know.

Always there other before, make, unmake me again.

Walking up the street last night,
the new moon looming like the pine trees' memory,
I walked into the shadows, the trees'
entanglements. Was I walking into you?

The light rises to wing-beat and dusk.
World runs in feather, fur, and scale, leaves and light.
Elsewhere always. Elsewhere place.
Here place. Now place.

No longer loam. No longer auditory.

THE OTHER

shone in moonlight, mirrored
all over the streets and store windows.
The rain came on. I took

to the trees and awnings around town.
Clouds gauzed the moon.
All I wanted was my archaic diction back.

I walked all night through the rain
trying to call the thing its proper other,
walked in fields and back to town.

Hasn't there been beauty enough?
Rain fell on the tin roof all day
like a new language coming on.

verbum

Word lived in solitude.
Walked the dog before dawn.
Coffee on the patio. The air was thin.
There were no stars.
Silence drifted from the river
with the mist. Word
wandered through the house,
looked out the window.

Could the darkness speak,
what would it say?
What would Word answer?
Word took a deep breath, yawned,
and spoke the beginning.

Spanned the darkness
in a single stride, sprawled
across the couch too exhausted
to speak, snored all afternoon,
woke with a bitter taste,
woke in the time of the human,

time of the archive speaking
beginnings into time. The time faded
and came back in a cloud bank
going gold then gray.
Time of the hall with mud floors.
Time of the sun.

Time of cathedral bells echoing the city.
Time of dust falling through the day.
Shining moon time.
Time ticking hands.
Time out of time just in time.
Crumbling bread. Heavy wine.

Word walked in the garden in the early evening,
waited in the desert, went into the city, wandered
along the winding streets, read the law,
roared, slept some more, stirred
in dreams—What shines in profusion there?—

upended tables, screamed
all over, received wounds, broke
into works and words, spoke tongues
on the back porch, nighthawks
diving, cicadas coming on.

Word spoke another's tongue—can I,
can I speak the holy time?
Lost time. Glowing digits time.
Dig in the dirt time.
That touch and taste.
Heavy bread. Heavy wine.

outlines, ashes, prayers

Something breathes in me open-mouthed, catching
at words I don't recognize save for
a word or two about hereafter, heavenward,
hammered like the balls we kicked
into the priest's buckeye tree, knocking
down seeds, eyes in my pockets
all the walk home, unseeing.

It was like this. I drew a straight flush and folded.
It was by the river, roiling fumes,
something hammering away under
a gray rock, that rock-colored gray,

                    and the signed life goes by,

othering, outering offspring,
    the air a dim glow,
some agreeing voice passing,
the right place passing its by,
yes by and going by.

Speak buttons to me, Jesus.
        Everything is whereas.
I tried painting the cinder blocks gold,
a dream of the cross and St. Michael's passing.
What do you believe happens when it all ends?
I think it's fallen pears, a rock garden,
sweet rot, buzzing flies,
a dark porch and storms coming.
Wings beating and all that coming on.
It's a time share, right?
Rot, rocks, and buzzing.

A Piece of Granite

Brother to these shelves and musty pages,
metallic illustrations, crows arrayed across the yard—
their struts, calls, and darting looks.
Beside the coffee maker, I breathe their shape.

My pillow is a stone.
My heart is work in paper and ink.

The crows illumine into a script I cannot read,
circle, and tap the roof, imitating rain.

Brother to this rain, I make my way
to the river where I become
a companion talking to the woods.

And brother to the distant bells.

DrIVING

Can't tell how all this works.
Wheels turn, and fires burn. What else?
I'm driving all over town
like zither music in my head

keeps me safe, and there you are
showing up, one craftwork
fair after another, glitter-covered,
glued together—cut-out figures

from construction paper. If only
I could remember you now the way
it was before everything came down,
settling on the TV sets

like snowstorms catching fire.
Where is that thing chased me all
the years, chasing years, that glitter-eyed
and flaming nothing, my friend?

PLACE, a STUDY

Lateral place. Dusk place.
After midnight place.

What is this coming to?
Let place fade again, this place
woven into no place.

Times converge, cross over.
Sand place. Hour place.
They come together, sunlight,
dusk, and dust.

Shift space, fallen space,
space cannot overcome itself.

Here the coffee steams, the radio plays,
pixels play out on screens.

Fellowship of clouds, of wings,
a murder, flock, or entertainment.
Place of hours.

Wings fall to darkness.
Let there be no place.
To darkness the world all comes.
To sound and the absence of sound.
Light and its other.
Yes, light and its other.

SHIFTING MOONLIGHT

In case I ever get past this thing I am
and speak, I'm forging new inflections late
at night, a voice in sleep, this couch,
this shaded room in a participled place.

I might as well give up the other that
stirs and murmurs me and all the past.
I've tried to change my language for so long,
the clerks announce my license has expired.

The offices are closed and boarded up.
The run-down marketplaces lower their prices.
I don't know what or when comes next.
I am your other, says the voice in sleep,

the moon, that valid moon, a place
of shaken air, the other you become,
a lonely, stretched-out thing holding instances
apart, where everybody, everybody gets in free.

Beginnings Again

A silver thread weaves through my hand,
gleams in lamplight, my hand flexing there,
the needle plunging into bleeding skin,
making a high-pitched sound, a silver sound
becoming sentences that speak into the dark,
speaking mown grass, raked grass,
hay bales as high as memory allows.

The words gleam in the flame.
Tarnished words converge into beginnings,
flame and words on the lawn
in moonlight, fairy rings and shining streaks
across the sky, the distant rumbling

entering a sentence that began elsewhere,
buzzing on my tongue, the tarnished thread,
the hand it pierces, hand it weaves.
The gleaming and nothing before.
The before it weaves. The after.

ABOUT THE AUTHOR

Jerry Harp grew up in southern Indiana, where he studied English at St. Meinrad College (BA), a seminary run by Benedictine monks. He went on to receive degrees from St. Louis University (MA), the University of Florida (MFA), and the University of Iowa (PhD), where he specialized in Renaissance literature. He has taught at prep schools in St. Louis and at Kenyon College, and he currently teaches at Lewis & Clark College in Portland, Oregon, where he lives with his wife, Mary Szybist, and their cat, Anime.

Acknowledgments

Poems appear in the following publications, sometimes in different forms or under different titles.

Best American Poetry 2009
Boulevard, Cincinnati Review
The Dirty Goat
Fulcrum
Image
The Iowa Review
The Journal
Kenyon Review
The Laurel Review
Notre Dame Review
The Oregonian, Pleiades
Poetry Daily website
Ruminate
Spoon River Poetry Review

Thank you for help and support to Eve Adamson, Dawn Corrigan, Jeff Hamilton, Gabriela Rife, Mike Smolinsky, Jason Sommer, and Mary Szybist.

ALSO BY Jerry Harp

POETRY

Creature (Salt Publishing, 2003)

Gatherings (Ashland Poetry Press, 2004)

Urban Flowers, Concrete Plains
(Salt Publishing, 2006)

NONFICTION

*Constant Motion: Ongian Hermeneutics and the
Shifting Ground of Early Modern Understanding*
(Hampton Press, 2010)

*For Us, What Music? The Life and Poetry of Donald
Justice* (U. of Iowa Press, 2010)

As co-editor: *A Poetry Criticism Reader*
(U. of Iowa Press, 2006)

NeoPoiesis: *a new way of making*

1) in ancient Greece, poiesis referred to the process of making: creation - production - organization - formation - causation

2) a process that can be physical and spiritual, biological and intellectual, artistic and technological, material and teleological, efficient and formal

3) a means of modifying the environment and a method of organizing the self, the making of art and music and poetry, the fashioning of memory and history and philosophy, the construction of perception and expression and reality

4) an independent publisher with a steadfast goal to print and promote outstanding poets, writers and artists who reflect the creative drive and spirit of the new electronic landscape

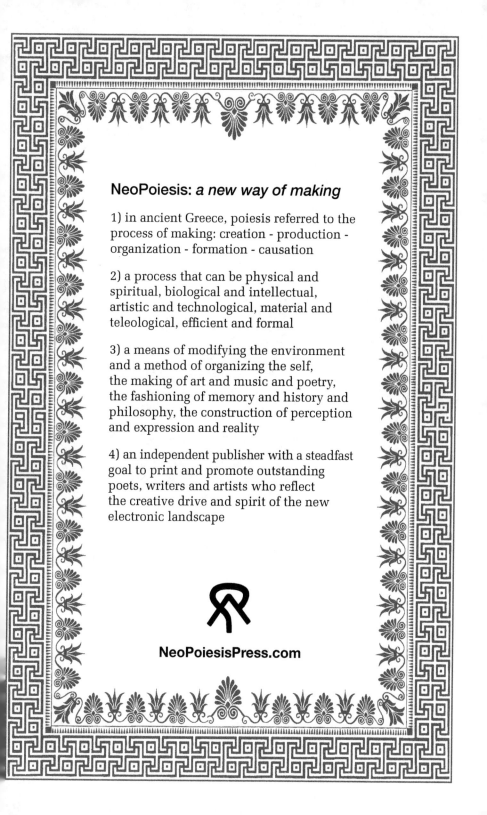

NeoPoiesisPress.com